The

UnderPass

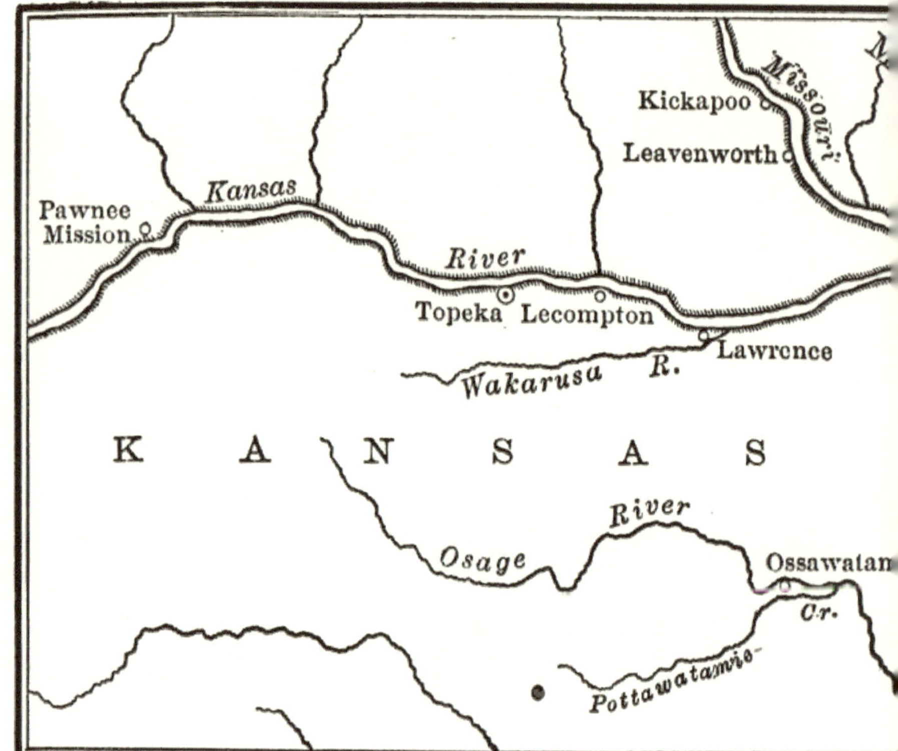

This is a work of fiction. Some of the events and some of the characters described herein are imaginary and are not intended to refer to specific places or living persons. The opinions expressed in this manuscript are solely the opinions of the author and do not represent the opinions of the publisher. The author has represented and warranted full ownership and/or legal right to publish all the materials in this book. Tonni "Pharoh" Fewell asserts the moral right to be identified as the author of this work.

The UnderPass

Fewell Media 2022

http://www.thepinnacleperspective.com

ISBN: 979-835-948-444-2

Library of Congress Number: TXu 2-325-599

PRINTED IN THE UNITED STATES OF AMERICA

This book is dedicated to all my Real Ones out there…You Know Who You Are!

"For Every Step that I take, You Take With Me, For Every Breath that I Take, You Take With Me" -Tupac Amaru Shakur (R.I.P)

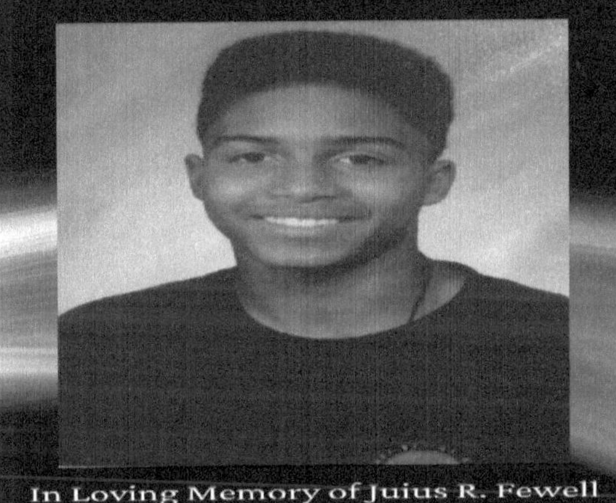
In Loving Memory of Juius R. Fewell
1978-2021
Love You, Miss You! 300%

PROLOGUE

July 1997, Ewingston, Missouri

"You better hurry up before they get you Juke!" is all I heard from one of the older boys running ahead of me. It was pitch black and we like many other adolescent boys our age were doing mischievous, sometimes reckless things during the summer of my freshman year of high school.

I am not exactly sure whose idea it was for us to go and visit the Old Dominion cemetery that night. This decrepit cemetery had been condemned for many years and was rumored to be haunted. Knowing us, it was probably an "I dare you" or "I bet you won't" challenge of young testosterone and nerve. I ran as fast as I could like someone was chasing me, I could feel the softness of the ground as I took each step. It felt as if this fertile ground underneath me could cave in at any moment.

I kept running faster and harder. Just as I was picking up a good pace, I tripped over a flat headstone that had been concealed within the ground cover and crashed and burned into the grass. "OUCH" I shouted. As soon as I went to get up, a sharp pain instantly shot straight down through my right leg.

Just then Marcus, one of the bigger, older boys that were running ahead of me, immediately turned around and picked me up. He proceeded to carry me for a while until I felt the pain had subsided and I was able to limp along on my own.

After a 50-yard scary cemetery dash, we made our way over the gate and into the car and quickly sped away. Once we got back into town, we all shared a sense of relief as we had survived the "haunted Old Dominion" cemetery dare at night.

I am not sure when or who it was that started the rumor of the Old Dominion Cemetery being a haunted place. All I know is that the kids in and around Ewingston, were frightful of that place and they steered clear of it. In addition to those local haunted rumors and superstitions, there was also another important reason why we were in such a hurry to get out of there.

It was because of some local attack dogs. Meet Smoky and Reno! Two of the most ferocious Doberman Pinschers you ever did see! These two dogs from hell came out only at night and would terrorize anyone foolish enough to roam around the grounds near the cemetery.

No one knew who their owners were. Most people in Ewingston, especially on my side of town, knew that after dark, you had better be prepared to run or risk being attacked by them. And if you ran from them, you had better be quick, because they were extremely fast and out for blood!

Those two vicious attack dogs did not discriminate against their victims, they would attack adults or children, it did not matter. Now that I am grown, I realized that someone intentionally let them out at night near our neighborhood to cause harm to us. Wow! That's crazy, right?

I

FOUNDATIONAL

Present Day, Free City, Ks

Hello, world! My name is Mr. Julius Richard Jeffrey aka "Juke." I am a local Tycoon and Civil Engineer. I own several profitable companies in the large metropolitan city known as Free City, Kansas. Free City or "First City" for short, is the first city you enter once you cross the bridge over the Missouri River, thus the name. With light traffic, Free City is about a half-hour drive west of my hometown of Ewingston, Missouri. Free City is a very progressive city with a diverse population of people from all over the country. I moved to Free City after graduate school and fell in love with the vibe of the city. I was particularly drawn to the various forms of Victorian architecture of the local houses in the area. Being close to my hometown was an added bonus, in which I could be close to my family, while still carving out my existence.

Some might consider me to be an eccentric bachelor. I will be that, but I prefer to be a more behind-the-scenes type of guy that takes advantage of the opportunities that come my way.

The companies that I own vary, they are mostly in the fields of Aerospace & Defense, Historical Exploration, Commercial and Residential Real Estate as well as a Civil Engineering consulting firm. I make it a point to surround myself with innovative people, whether they be young or old. You never are too old or too young to learn or to teach!

Although I hold a master's degree in civil engineering, I also own a very prominent exploration business called "First Find". We seek to find lost and rare historical treasures, facts, and little-known information all over the globe.

I have been a treasure hunter ever since I can remember. I am very passionate about closing those open chapters of historical events and educating people on the hidden histories of the people, places, and events lost in time.

As a kid, I owned two metal detectors. I was always outside, exploring things. I found everything in my neighborhood from old, rusted soda cans to various scrap items and even some old civil war bullets. One day when I was about thirteen years old while searching an area near the Old Dominion cemetery, I found ten rare solid gold coins, which netted me a nice profit I must say!

Since I do not have any siblings, my loving parents Richard and Deanne Jeffrey, spoiled me, they pretty much provided me with anything that I ever wanted growing up. It was kind of cool being an only child, of course, I would get lonely sometimes, but I always found a way to entertain myself.

One advantage that I had over some of my peers was the fact that both of my parents are successful, respected educators in our community. My father is an esteemed professor of Political Science, and my mother is a professor emeritus of Economics at the local Historical Black College known as Gabriel Prosser University. This storied institution is proudly named in honor of the brave Black American blacksmith turned revolutionary Mr. Gabriel Prosser (Bowen 2021).

Prosser and the other revolt conspirators were more than likely influenced by the recent American Revolution as well as the French and Haitian Revolutions. Inspired by those events, Prosser began to put together a plot to create a massive slave rebellion in Richmond, Virginia on August 30th,1800. In the words of one of the leaders of the American Revolution named Patrick Henry, it was going to be "Freedom or Death," that was the mindset. No

Retreat, No Surrender!

Over a short amount of time, Prosser eventually

attracted several other like-minded slaves to assist him in

his rebellion. Since most of them worked in the fields, this

group of slaves along with Gabriel began to gather

whatever agricultural instruments they could get their

hands on to be used as weapons for the rebellion.

The group also started making swords in preparation

to attack and make their escape. Prosser planned to initiate

his rebellion on the night of August 30. As fate would have

it, earlier that day there was a big rainstorm which caused

a delay in their revolutionary plans. After the storm ended, two of the loyal slaves of the plantation, who wanted to

protect their masters, exposed the plot to the Virginia

authorities.

Prosser was able to flee and avoided capture for

about a month or so after the plot was exposed. He was

eventually apprehended and was hung along with several

of his co-conspirators after a speedy public trial on

October 6, 1800 (Bowen, 2021).

I am a proud alumnus of that illustrious college

because my parents wanted me to remain close to home

while in college. It was cool though because I never had to

live in the dorms nor have to pay for an apartment, Sweet!

Over the years my admiration for adventure and

history along with my relentless pursuit of finding lost or

hidden treasures has taken me to many places all around

the world. However, the adventure that I am about to speak of began a long, long time ago in a nearby place.

Let me give you a little background. My hometown is a place called Ewingston, Missouri. This is your typical Midwestern town. It is located west of the Missouri River, which acts as an invisible border between Missouri and Kansas.

Growing up, I never could understand why there was always such a rivalry between these two states that border each other. In addition to the well-known long-standing rivalry of sports between the University of Missouri versus the University of Kansas, this place also holds significance to the American Civil War. Later on, I would find out why.

In 1860, the United States of America was on the brink of a Civil War. The spark that ignited the flame began in the areas in and around Missouri and Kansas. Originally known as "An Act to Organize the Territories of Nebraska and Kansas." Signed into law in 1854 by President Franklin Pierce, the Kansas-Nebraska Act repealed the Missouri Compromise of 1820 (Kerrihard, 1999).

The Missouri Compromise legally allowed slavery in the territories north of the 36 degrees by thirty latitudes, this imaginary line ran directly below both Missouri and Kansas.

Created by Illinois senator Stephen Douglas, the Kansas-Nebraska Act, would impose that the people of each territory would determine the institution of slavery, also known as popular sovereignty (Kerrihard, 1999).

After the Kansas-Nebraska Act passed in Congress, violence erupted between the pro-slavery Missourians and the "Jayhawkers" of the free state of Kansas. This issue resulted in many years of local election fraud instances, brutal state-line crossing raids, and fights, in addition to several revenge murders. These acts, whether simple scuffles or cold-blooded murders, were the unfortunate fruits of long-standing, bitter seeds that had been planted many years before. (Kerrihard, 1999).

A key figure in the Missouri Vs. Kansas border conflict was the ardent American abolitionist, John Brown. Originally from Connecticut, this courageous anti-slavery advocate believed in using whatever violent means necessary to end the inhumane institution of American chattel slavery immediately. Brown's edict was *"I have only a short time to live, only one death to die, And I will die fighting for this cause."* Truer words were never spoken, in my opinion.

Brown had plans to participate in a massive slave insurrection in order to bring his vision of freedom for all by any means to fruition. (Horwitz, 2011). Brown arrived in the Kansas territory in 1855 in a covered wagon loaded with ammunition and weapons. Accompanying him were five of his sons. Brown settled near Osawatomie, KS, and stayed with the Adair family of that area.

While in Osawatomie, he was instrumental in gathering and rallying the anti-slavery forces to stand against the pro-slavery forces just across the border in Missouri (Horwitz, 2011).

As a response to the sacking of Lawrence, Ks by the pro-slavery forces, Brown led a small band of his men into Pottawatomie, Ks on May 24, 1856. Once there, his men drug several pro-slavery proponents from their homes and executed them. After this, Brown led raids into Missouri-freeing many slaves and killing their owners (Horwitz, 2011).

By the fall of 1856, Brown left Kansas with three of his five sons and returned back East to aid in the northern abolitionist movement there. The impact of John Brown's game-changing presence in the Missouri-Kansas area worked as a double-edged sword, unfortunately. He inspired the local people who immediately wanted to end slavery by any means necessary. While in contrast, he enraged those who were in favor of continuing slavery, as he was the antithesis of their unjust justification of it (Horwitz, 2011).

II

DOWN HOME

Present Day Ewingston, Mo

Finally, the Thanksgiving weekend had arrived. I took off for about a week or so from my daily duties, and I decided that I was going to visit my parents and some of my friends back in Ewingston. When I reached my hometown, it was getting dark out, so I headed over to my parent's house.

Walking in through the front door I heard my mother say, "There's my boy" along with my father's usual "Hey son how you are doing?" and their welcoming warm embraces. I greeted them both and said, "Hi Mom, Hi Dad, Love you" and we hugged as if we had not seen each other in the flesh in a little while.

You know it is amazing how we claim to be so busy with our daily lives, that we neglect spending time with those closest to us sometimes, most importantly our parents, but I digress.

Anyway, it felt great to be home once again. Since I had moved out of my parent's house long ago, they turned my old bedroom upstairs into a guest room. I did not mind though, I just hoped that the bed was just as comfortable as I remember it being back when I lived there. Ahhh, Yes it was!

I was a little exhausted from work and the drive, so I laid down and took me a little power nap before we ate dinner. When I awoke, I went downstairs and who did I see? My other two favorite humans, none other than my beloved grandparents!

My grandfather Julius, who is my namesake, is an amazing man. Originally from Temecula, California, He was also a successful businessman/engineer in his time. In addition to that, he was also a war hero, having proudly served in Vietnam as a fighter pilot. He was even awarded the Air Force Cross for valor during battle. His beautiful, better half is my wonderful grandmother Georgia, she is impressive in her own right as well. She originates from historic St. Augustine, Florida.

My grandmother Georgia is a direct descendant of the great Black Seminole Maroons of that area. Her parents were Native and Black. "Maroons," are the descendants of the Black people who fled into Florida and the Carolinas and mixed in with the Indigenous tribes to escape European colonization, slavery, and disease. These "Black Maroons" became warriors in their own right.

They were able to survive by their own means and formed many independent communities in the swamps and other areas where they were not likely to be found by the colonizers.

In addition to this remarkable independent spirit, these American Maroons also continuously fought the U.S. government from forcibly taking their homelands during the 19th Century (Alexander, 2022).

My grandparents have always been an excellent resource when it comes to our family's history along with many other Foundational Black American historical little-known facts.

What is a Foundational Black American you might ask? A Foundational Black American is a non-immigrant Black person who is a descendant of the formerly enslaved people here in America. FBA as we are sometimes referred to can also trace our lineage to the Indigenous people that have lived in America for thousands of years (Nasheed, 2021) before Christopher Columbus arrived.

FBA origins go back to the year of 1526 when the Spanish magistrate and conquistador Lucas Vazquez de Ayllon brought over a group of black Moors from Spain to the New World. Ayllon and his six hundred troops settled in the modern-day area of South Carolina as well as in the Georgia Atlantic coastal region. These enslaved black moors waged a triumphant rebellion against the Spaniards.

This rebellion ultimately forced the Spanish to have to evacuate. After this occurred, these newly liberated Black people then integrated with the local Native American tribes in the area and created their own communities and cultures as a result.

I can vividly remember myself, my parents, and my grandparents going to a family reunion down in Florida when I was in middle school. I remember we visited a place called *Fort Mose* (pronounced Mo-Say). This was the first free Black settlement established in 1738 north of Saint Augustine, Florida.

Fort Mose mostly consisted of the Black and Native people of that area. The fort began to flourish and became a beacon of hope for the many escaped slaves that had made it there from the nearby slaveholding states.

My grandmother taught me that the original underground railroad led to Florida, as Florida was a colony of Spain. Many fugitive slaves sought refuge in the many marshes and swamps throughout the Florida, as well as The Great Dismal Swamp, which covers the Virginia and North Carolina borders.

Around 1808, Spain outlawed slavery in its colonies, except in Cuba. Spain would grant freedom to the many blacks and natives, in exchange for their loyalty to the Spanish crown and their conversion to Catholicism.

When word got out about this nearby freedom land, many enslaved blacks as well as many fleeing Native Americans from different tribes began escaping into Florida.

Unfortunately, the United States began to expand further into the South and therefore began encroaching into Florida. Forces led by General Andrew Jackson invaded Spanish Florida, and attacked key locations, and pushed the Seminoles and Black Maroons further south into the Florida Everglades.

The Seminoles and their Black counterparts fought bravely and made the invading US troops even have to retreat on several occasions using guerrilla warfare tactics. Eventually, the US troops began to prevail in their efforts through the use of their advanced weaponry. They forced

the natives to have to migrate.

This forced migration eventually led to the Seminole

Wars that lasted from 1816 to 1858. This always gave me

a sense of pride knowing that the people of my lineage

were resilient and stood up for themselves against

oppression, colonization, and tyranny (Diouf, 2022).

I have always enjoyed spending time with my

grandparents, they have always been there for me and

continue to be a guiding light to not only my parents but

for me as well. Both are retired and have been for quite a

while now, so they spend most of their time traveling

throughout the continental USA in their state-of-the-art custom RV.

It was now dinner time! A delicious combination of my father's famous hickory smoked brisket, and my mother's cheesy potatoes, asparagus, and baked beans made for a legendary supper! That meal definitely reminded me of the good ole days for real! For dessert, my grandmother's classic triple chocolate mousse pie a la mode with vanilla ice cream and sprinkles hit the spot like it always does!

Full as a tick, from our great supper mixed with dessert, my father, grandfather, and I headed out on my parents' veranda. We fired up some exclusive Cuban cigars, poured up a few glasses of my father's imported premium Scotch Whiskey, and began talking some more.

For some odd reason, the old story of me and my friends braving the challenge of running across the Old Dominion Cemetery at night came up during our conversation.

I explained to them how foolish it was for us teens to be out there at night trying to prove to each other that we were not afraid of anything. Although most of us kids were indeed afraid at that moment, we just did not want to show it at the time. Especially since other than the rumored ghosts in the cemetery, two other threats were also lurking about, i.e., Smoky and Reno!

My grandfather then began telling us the hidden history of the Old Dominion cemetery as well as an impromptu history lesson. Originally the cemetery was created to bury the deceased slaves in the area during

Antebellum slavery. After slavery was "abolished" in America, a new wave of laws came into effect known as "Black Codes". These laws were passed in response to the abolition of slavery.

These black codes restricted Black people in where they could live, work, or even vote. These black codes were in addition to the State government-enforced Jim Crow laws that were created in 1877 and lasted until the 1960s.

Originally started as a minstrel show, the character known as "Jim Crow" eventually turned into a series of segregation laws and practices throughout America with the misleading motto of "Separate but equal." This led to many towns being segregated based on race, not only in the South but also in the North.

It is common knowledge or law among the locals, about the invisible boundaries that exist, that you better not cross, especially after dark. And as with most towns in those days, Ewingston was no exception to this rule.

Ewingston is a segregated town, in which all the Black folks live on the East side of town and all the white folks live on what is known as the West End. The Old Dominion cemetery is located in the southeastern part of town, closer to the eastern part.

After my grandfather's history lesson, I became intrigued! I had only known of the Old Dominion cemetery from the local rumors and superstitions in addition to that crazy night when my friends and I were running through it as wild youths. Other than that, most townspeople avoided that place because it was run down, with weeds growing all over the tombstones and fences, even covering up the old iron cut-out sign that read "Old Dominion 1840" on the main gate.

"Please continue Grandpa," I said as I remembered back when I would sit on his lap, and he would read me those enchanting bedtime stories as a young child.

These stories passed down from my grandfather and grandmother were always so fascinating to me. I would drift off to sleep and dream of all those adventures they told me about and wonder what it would have been like to live in those times.

III

THE LEGEND

My grandfather continued, "What many townspeople around here do not know is, the legend of the

Bomaki diamonds." "Huh, what is that?" I asked. He continued, "According to folklore, these precious stones were originally stolen by a Portuguese slave trader from the small village of Bo near the Sewa River in Sierra Leone, West Africa from a naïve young prince named Bomaki."

He went on "Prince Bomaki was embroiled in a bloody tribal war in the year 1825." "Prince Bomaki was eventually set up and murdered by a rival tribe during this conflict. After that occurred, the slave traders proceeded to savagely plunder his village, kill anyone who resisted, and take everything that they thought had some value."

"During this plunder, they came across a cache of rare emerald, green diamonds that had been hidden in the prince's treasury. After this occurred, the slavers loaded up the human cargo i.e., kidnapped Africans, some gallons of rum, and some other supplies, and they proceeded to sail west for America."

He went on "Upon arrival in America, the Africans who survived the horrors of the Middle Passage were quickly unloaded off the ships in shackles and then sold at slave auctions along with the rum and other items stolen from the motherland."

"Approximately 12.5 million people in total were taken from Africa." He said. "Wow, that's crazy," I said looking over at my father. I had never heard of this story before. "Keep going Grandpa," I said, then I turned to my father. My father looked back at me and replied that he had heard about the legend also as a kid from not only my grandparents but a few of the other elders around town.

My grandfather continued on with the story, "Rumor has it that just like how the slave traders forcibly stole the diamonds, Karma came back around, and the people who stole the diamonds were eventually strongarmed, killed, and robbed of 'Em." My grandfather then said in closing, "They never did find those stones, no one ever knew what came of them, but they are out there somewhere, yes indeed" he said as he shook his head. We finished our conversation and then headed back inside the house to visit with each other some more and play some board games as a family.

After the Thanksgiving weekend, when I returned to my office. I was so inspired and consumed by the story my grandfather had told me and my father. Right then, I decided to make it my mission to find out more about the legend based on my grandfather's story about it.

I immediately instructed my operations team to begin thoroughly researching the history of Ewingston, The Old Dominion Cemetery, and The Legend of the Bomaki diamonds.

In tandem with that, I began reaching out to some of my colleagues that owed me some favors in the historical exploration industry for some information, resources, and data. After a few days of digging, the information that my team provided was both limited as well as possibly fruitful, maybe. Could be useful, I thought.

In addition to the information that I received from my trusted resources, I did some investigating of my own, I started interviewing some of the local elders in and around Ewingston. I was able to find out some information about the characters in the story.

I found out there was a man by the name of Whitney Stevenson. He was a wealthy southern landowner and slave trader, who had relocated his family and slaves from Louisiana to Missouri. I thought to myself, Wow! This was the dude that my Grandpa Julius was talking about at my parent's house that night!

There was another character in the story. He was a notorious Portuguese slave trader named Santiago Adelaberta. He would travel back and forth from the Eastern seaboard to the Upper South states, transporting and delivering slaves.

I found out that there were two different versions of how Stevenson ended up with the Bomaki diamonds. One story which is the most common, tells how a young

Whitney Stevenson found out about the diamonds that Santiago was holding and robbed and killed him for them.

There was also a second tale that many local people were unaware of, which tells the story of how Santiago had squandered all his money away on women and booze after one of his big "deliveries." He had become desperate, so much so that he wagered all the diamonds in a high-stakes poker game and lost it all.

Whitney Stevenson, who was a frequent customer of Santiago's human merchandise, as well as a well-known card shark, recognized this and became the one who ended up winning the diamonds in that card game.

I am not sure exactly which one of these stories is true. But one of them had to be, I hoped for history's sake.

Regardless, the Legend of the Bomaki diamonds was a very intriguing story and I wanted to find out if there was any truth to it! I believe legends like this really took place in many small American towns and Ewingston was no different.

Many young boys and girls dream of being the one person who discovers a little-known treasure or being the one to solve a well-known mystery that no one else could. This was my passion as a youngster. I loved exploring creeks and making trails in the woods, looking for various kinds of wildlife and plants.

If I found something that I thought was either unique or cool, I would take it home to my parents. Together we would place the items under a microscope and closely examine them to determine exactly what it was and where they could have come from. Learning about the many forms of wildlife in the area, equipped me with keen attention to detail as well as some survival skills while adding to my passion for adventure and knowledge.

There are many things in nature and life, in general, that could prove useful if used properly. Of course, common sense comes into play in most situations, like being aware of your surroundings. Sometimes you just have to Stop, Look and Listen. Some answers may not always be obvious at first but can be revealed over time. Using my internal instincts has always been helpful to me in whatever it was that I was studying.

IV

REASONS

1859 Ewingston, Mo

Whitney Stevenson was the largest landowner and

slave owner in all of St. George's County, Missouri, with

Ewingston being the county seat. St. George's County is in

a section in the northwestern area of Missouri known as

"Little Dixie." Although, the climate in Missouri is not conducive to growing cotton, which was the cash crop of the south. Many of the plantations in that area, mostly cultivated hemp and tobacco farms.

Whitney Stevenson's large plantation produced both items. He authorized land to be allotted to bury his slaves on the grounds, near his mansion. This became known as "The Old Dominion Cemetery."

He was also rumored to be a member of the infamous Knights of the Golden Circle. This was a clandestine organization founded before the Civil War in 1859 by a con man named George Bickley (William, Roush 2005). Bickley created the first *castle*, or local branch in Cincinnati, Ohio. Although created in the North, the order spread into the South, where it was well-received.

Their nefarious objective was to create a "golden circle" consisting of the upper south states as well as many parts of the southern United States including Mexico. This also included some Caribbean countries.

Their mission was to uphold the so-called "southern way of life", and to further continue the horrible institution of chattel slavery (William, Roush 2005).

Some of the rumored members of the Knights of the Golden Circle also known as the KGC are a few famous names in American history. This secret societal organization included John Wilkes Booth and his co-conspirators in the Lincoln assassination, other members include Confederate President Jefferson Davis, and infamous Missouri outlaws Frank and Jesse James (William, Roush 2005).

This "new country" that the KGC proposed and dreamed of would have been headquartered in Havana, Cuba. Their vision was for the new territories admitted to the United States would be annexed into the Confederate States of America. This would increase the number of slaveholding states over the non-slaveholding states which would add to their political sphere of influence.

One of Stevenson's recently purchased field slaves was a beautiful young Native American, and Black female he named Madeline, nicknamed Maddie. She had been forcibly captured from the Otoe tribe in Nebraska in a brutal slave-snatching raid. Her father was an escaped slave named John from Texas whom the tribe had taken in.

While living amongst the Otoe tribe, John met and fell and love with Maddie's mother, a beautiful woman by the name of Onatah. She was named after a Native American corn goddess, which means "Of the Earth."

Maddie was close to her mother Onatah, as she became her sole parent after her father was murdered during the murderous raid on her village. Onatah was also captured and sold into slavery in the deep south. Maddie would never see her mother again. This really saddened Maddie because her mother was her idol and had meant everything to her.

Because of this and a few other reasons, Maddie harbored a deep-seated hatred for not only Whitney Stevenson but also for the wicked institution of slavery. She loathed performing her daily duties and was traumatized by the many terrible things that she had encountered in her life while being a field slave. The beatings, the disrespect, the pain. Enough was enough she thought.

Maddie had always yearned to be free and began plotting with several other of Stevenson's field slaves on escaping. She was born free and wanted to regain that feeling as an adult. She felt she had nothing to lose. A plan was then enacted. All of the slaves, four in total including two men and two women initiated a plan to escape during the upcoming Stevenson plantation's annual 4th of July jubilee.

Their escape was to occur while the Stevenson's and their guests were ironically celebrating the United States winning its freedom from Great Britain's rule. The Stevenson plantation always held a large ball on the night of the 4th of July every year which included massive fireworks displays, cooking, and dancing.

Maddie knew that the Stevenson's and their guests were more than likely going to be preoccupied with all the festivities taking place. Therefore, the overseers would be a little more lax than normal.

While the 4th of July celebration was going on could present a perfect opportunity for them to escape. There was a chance that they would not be noticed missing until after the plantation overseers did their daily slave headcount the next day. This would also give Maddie and the others enough time to put as much distance between them and the Stevenson plantation.

Their plan was then set into motion. Maddie had been conspiring with a few others that were going to stay on at the plantation. Unfortunately, they would have to endure the worst of Stevenson's brutal punishments and torture in response to the few slaves that had escaped.

Originally, Maddie planned to escape during the Christmas and New Year's holidays. During this time, some slaves were allowed by their owners to go and visit their nearby family and friends, which could present a great opportunity for them to make a run for it and never return. However, Maddie eventually scrapped this escape idea, because of the brutally cold Midwestern winters in Missouri and Kansas. It would be nearly impossible for her to travel if there was a snowstorm or if the ground was frozen solid. It is hard to run fast on ice!

The main person that Maddie had been speaking to whom she knew she could trust was her dear friend Hattie. Hattie was one of the house slaves that the Stevenson family trusted. She also shared in Maddie's desire to one day be free.

Many of the slaves of the Stevenson plantation had heard the rumors of Whitney's highly coveted African diamonds, and they had figured more than likely they were stashed somewhere inside the big house.

The plan was for Hattie to find a way to steal the Bomaki diamonds while the 4th of July festivities were in full swing and very quickly and discreetly have them delivered to Maddie before her great escape.

Regardless of the upcoming holiday, it still was business as usual at the Stevenson plantation. All the slaves performed their daily labors and chores as expected, showing no signs of a pending escape plot. The time was drawing near.

V

PLAN, PLOT, AND STRATEGIZE

1859 Ewingston, Mo

To escape from slavery, one must consider a few crucial factors. Careful planning, timing, and diligence were the key ingredients, but the most important aspect of any plot is secrecy. Remember, Loose lips sink ships!

Being able to keep a secret is a vital component to not only a successful escape but also for survival while on the journey. Keeping your mouth shut is the key. If some of the loyal house slaves and even a few of the field slaves got wind of a pending escape plot, they would not hesitate to squeal to the master, hoping to gain his favor or maybe even an extra butter biscuit or two.

Fortunately for Maddie and her group, the Stevenson Plantation was located not far from the border of the free state of Kansas. All they had to do was make it to the river and find a way across it. However, there were many slave catchers, known as the "paddy rollers" lurking around on patrol up and down the border looking for any

fugitive slaves.

The events of Maddie escaping from the Stevenson

plantation were rumored to have taken place around 1859.

Nine years earlier in 1850, The United States Congress

passed the second Fugitive Slave Act. Heavily supported

by the Southerners, this was a newly enacted federal law.

Unfortunately, this was the law of the land, therefore

fugitive slaves if captured were not considered U.S.

citizens or even human and had no rights in any court of

law. A fugitive slave could not dispute the legality of any

accusations placed upon them whatsoever (Augustyn,

2020).

If caught the fugitive slave faced getting torn to pieces by the vicious attack dogs, followed by a very painful public whipping from the overseers at the plantation. This was immediately be followed by the slave being sold to the deep south where even more brutal slave owners and daily torture methods awaited their arrival (Augustyn, 2020).

One of the worst of those aforementioned paddy rollers was the bloodthirsty Kilgore. Adam Kilgore was a dirt-poor, illiterate young man recently up from the deep south, who did not hesitate to use violence to keep Black people "in their place." Over the years, Kilgore had grown envious of the wealthy slave owners and their lifestyle, because he could never afford to purchase any slaves of his own or live as they lived.

This warped sense of reality stirred up resentment in him because he was looked down upon by those wealthy people as not being much better than the Black people he was chasing.

So, it was a big roll of the dice to escape, the stakes were high! You could either escape and hit the jackpot of freedom or you could crap out and find yourself in a horrible situation, possibly worse than before. Especially if you were to get caught by Kilgore and his cronies, they were brutal.

Even though Maddie's journey was not a long journey to freedom, it was not without the element of danger. They all had nothing to lose! A sense of urgency combined with the spirit toward liberty or death was enough motivation for this perilous journey to freedom not to seem that far after all for anyone brave enough to embark on it.

As I mentioned earlier, one advantage that Maddie had was that she had been born free. Because of this, she vaguely had a sense of what life felt like to not be held in bondage. And she yearned for that feeling so badly.

Maddie had spent her earliest years in the Nebraska territory with the Otoe tribe of that area. One night, her village was raided and destroyed by a squad of slave traders posing as U.S. Troops. Most of the men of her tribe including her father John were slaughtered.

The women and children were rounded up and forcibly taken away and sold into slavery, including her mother Onatah, and a few of her relatives in the tribe.

Luckily for Maddie, she was very sharp, even at an early age. She remembered the many valuable survival techniques that her tribe had instilled into her that would prove to be valuable later in her life, particularly at this juncture.

Before her name was changed to Maddie Stevenson, the name given to her by her parents at birth was *Yareli* which translates to "Water Lady" in the Otoe language. Her mother Onatah gave her that name because she was born near the Nishnabotna River, and ironically, she always loved to swim in that river as a young child.

VI

A LITTLE DEEPER

1859 Ewingston, Mo

The month of July had arrived, and as usual, it was miserably humid and muggy. Those who were set to escape from the Stevenson plantation, were Maddie of course, along with a young couple named Dwight and Ethel, as well as the beautiful young Dovie Ann. She was to be joining the rest of the slaves on their freedom mission as she was escaping from the nearby Bruner plantation.

The more I dug into the story of Maddie, Whitney Stevenson, and The Legend of the Bomaki diamonds, the more fascinated I became. I also noticed that some of the townspeople especially at the local library in Ewingston were standoffish to me when I began inquiring about the legend.

Also, I began noticing that there were several mysterious-looking white vans following me when I traveled to certain places around town. I was not exactly sure who it could be.

Could it be the descendants of Whitney Stevenson? Could it be the descendants of the Knights of the Golden Circle? The Feds? Either way, I caught on to them very quickly and decided to make it extremely hard for them to track my movements.

One of the first things that I did, since I owned several vehicles, was to not drive any of my vehicles, especially my recently purchased baby blue 2022 Bentley Bentayga S around town. I started having a different driver pick me up in different vehicles, at the many places that I frequented.

This was purposely done to throw whoever was off my trail. Sometimes I would be in a rental car, sometimes I would not be. I was also able to have my second in command, a brother named Dante, who closely resembled me, function as my body double. In addition to that, I was also connected to a couple of folks who specialized in IT. I had them get me a high-speed secure laptop and a 5G cell phone with an untraceable masked IP address. These devices would send out false signal locations to anyone tracking me. Thanks to my assets I was able to dig deeper into the story and find more unknown facts about the

legend.

VII

IF YOU STAY READY

July 4, 1859, Ewingston, Mo

According to my research, I found out that Maddie

was forward-thinking in her escape. I was able to find out

about the story of Maddie's escape from one of my

resources and it was a little something like this. Maddie

had set in motion a few things before taking off. One of the main things that Maddie did was to find out where Whitney Stevenson kept the keys to his coveted treasure inside his desk. Stevenson was very suspicious of everyone, including his own family.

Because of this, he hid the keys to the chest in various places throughout the house at various times. However, Hattie had been spying on him inconspicuously and was able to find out some of the various places in the house where he put the keys. Knowing this, Hattie constantly kept Maddie informed on the latest happenings and movements going on inside the big house. The Stevensons had no idea that they were going to be minus a few of their slaves after the 4th of July festivities. So, the stage was set, and the slaves all agreed that they would make their daring escape during the annual Stevenson July 4th celebration.

They would also meet up with young Dovie Ann Bruner and would all set out on their journey in search of freedom together. As I mentioned earlier, their journey to freedom was not extremely far like say from Florida to Delaware, it still had its fair share of challenges.

The Missouri River acts as an invisible border to Kansas and was patrolled heavily, which meant Maddie and the others could not trust anyone along their way. However, there was also a hidden advantage for some of the escaping slaves if they paid attention.

In contrast to the slave patrols lurking around the border, there were also a few Black Freedmen that worked along the many docks of the river. If given the opportunity, they would aid people in their escapes if they could recognize a certain code of language. They had to be extremely discreet as they never knew who was watching or listening. One slip-up could be disastrous for both the escaping slaves and the Freedmen.

Since it was July and the during this time the Midwest is known for its extremely hot summers. A few code words began to develop amongst the Freedmen and the escaping slaves.

One of the codes was the word "Blazing". If one of the Freedmen commented "It sure is hot out today" someone who knew the code would instantly recognize this and would reply to them using a similar descriptive term in a sentence like "Yes indeed, it is blazing out today".

Using this code word would immediately let both people know what time it was and what they needed to do when or if the time was right. News of these Black Freedmen assisting fugitive slaves to gain their freedom was witnessed by young Dovie Ann.

She saw this in action while she was on an errand from the Bruner plantation with her mother to the northern river town of Copperville. In addition to the Freedmen, many great abolitionists also aided in many slave escapes. But of course, you cannot have good without bad, unfortunately, there were also many Paddy rollers who were posing as abolitionists.

Being deceptive, these fake abolitionists would go out of their way to attempt to help an escaped slave, and at the last minute, Got Cha! They would aggressively restrain that person and immediately place shackles around their legs and wrists, and off they go, back to the plantation or to a nearby slave auction.

The 4th of July holiday had finally arrived at the Stevenson plantation. And the collective mood was generally festive and patriotic, with American flags flying everywhere along with the red, white, and blue decorations all over the place.

It was nearing evening and the sun had set, and all the guests were arriving in their horse-drawn carriages, most of them being slave owners and slave traders themselves from nearby plantations and farms.

Maddie, along with the others had been planning their escape for months. They had been patiently waiting and had planned every detail of their escape down to the minute. Everyone was ready and the stage was finally set for their great escape to freedom.

While the Stevenson's were enjoying themselves along with their guests, Maddie and her people were moving their escape plan into motion. Eavesdropping on a recent conversation between Whitney Stevenson and another local slave owner, Hattie was able to find out the details of the 4th of July activities. There was to be a large dinner followed by a fireworks display and then a ball.

This celebration created a perfect opportunity for an escape! Hattie was also able to find the secret compartment in Stevenson's desk where he kept the diamonds in his study.

The night proceeded as scheduled with a large seafood dinner and dessert, a fireworks display, and the ball taking place. Stevenson's study was located upstairs in the massive mansion and was currently unoccupied as all the guests were eating and dancing in the main ballroom.

Moving very stealthy, quickly, and carefully, Hattie snuck away from the main ballroom activities and crept up the stairs to Stevenson's study. She was able to find the latest spot where Stevenson had placed the keys earlier in the week. She was able to locate the secret compartment inside the hidden slot inside the desk. She then unlocked the drawer and retrieved a wooden box that contained the diamonds and quickly got out of there before anyone at the party even noticed her missing.

Hattie quickly made her way back down the staircase and into the main ballroom where all the festivities were happening and slipped right back into place as if she had never left.

After a lavish dinner and dessert had been served by the house slaves and consumed by the party, everybody headed outside to the front lawn for the fireworks display that was about to take place.

Sadie Stevenson, who was the mistress of the plantation rudely demanded Hattie "Girl, go fetch us some more wine from the kitchen now". Hattie jumped at the opportunity! "Yes Ma'am, Right Away," she replied. She immediately headed back inside the house into the kitchen, along with another one of the female house slaves named Lois and proceeded to replenish the wine as instructed.

VIII

LAUNCH

July 4, 1859, Ewingston, Mo

While in the kitchen, Hattie distracted Lois for a few seconds, just enough time for her to place the box, wrapped in a brown burlap bag, into the waste container that was to be taken out immediately by one of the male slaves working in the house, named Henry.

Henry was one of those suspicious house negroes foolishly loyal to the master, that I spoke of earlier, and had been designated by the Stevenson's to take out the kitchen garbage that night. And he was on his job that night…so he thought. Henry was focused and alert as he was taking out the garbage. He intently gazed around in all directions making sure there were not any strange happenings afoot.

After he was content that there was nothing out of the ordinary going on outside, he slowly returned back inside the house to continue on with his serving and garbage duties.

Watching Henry return inside, Maddie was able to quickly retrieve the bag out of the trash and place it inside her knapsack with the few other belongings that she cared to take with her on the journey.

Maddie, Dwight, and Ethel had planned every step to the" T "and had taken the necessary precautions to get as far away from that wicked place as quickly as possible. As Maddie headed back to meet up with the others, she began to reflect on a few of the things that had occurred in her rough young life up until that point. She remembered what it felt like to be free and was going to take this opportunity to make it a reality, whether it was now or never! She wondered what ever became of her village, her mother, and her people.

She reminisced back to the time right before her village was raided and destroyed. She remembered one night in particular that could have very easily ended tragically.

While Maddie and Onatah were returning back to their village from a trading mission with another one of the local tribes, The Pawnee, something fateful occurred. As the two were walking along the path through the timber, Onatah noticed a large dark creature approaching the two of them.

Acting on pure motherly protective instinct, Onatah immediately snatched Maddie up and quietly moved both of them inside a large bush thicket. Luckily, it was nighttime, so this thicket was well hidden in the tall grass and therefore not fully visible to whatever was coming their way.

Under the glow of the moonlight, they saw what it was, it was a large black panther! The big cat crept by slowly through the tall weeds, not ten feet from where they were hiding. Maddie and her mother immediately froze in their tracks! Nervously, silently, and patiently, they waited until the panther went away as suddenly as it had appeared.

Whoa, that was way too close! thought Maddie.

Maddie remembered how close her mother had clenched onto her and held her finger over her mouth, whispering "Shush" very softly as their lives were in imminent danger should the panther notice them and want to attack.

She longed to have children of her own someday. And just as her mother had done for her, she knew that she would do whatever was necessary to protect her children from any danger.

Meanwhile, ironically just as Whitney Stevenson was proposing his "God Bless the Great Nation of America, Let Freedom Ring!" toast with his family and guests, four of his slaves were about to escape at that very moment!

Maddie, Dwight, and Ethel met up with young Dovie Ann, in the woods near the plantation, and under the cover of darkness, their journey toward the sweet taste of freedom had now begun. This was the moment that they had all waited for! I am sure there was a collective thought among all of them of the possibilities of being free and all the things that would come with it.

More than likely, the fear of being caught was also ever-present in this situation. But this was a risk that was worth taking! No more cruel masters, No more whippings, no more manual labor for no pay, No more pain, No more Fear! It was time to go and never look back thought Maddie!

Present Day Free City, Ks

As I continued to gather and compile all the information about the legend, I was extra careful as I mentioned earlier in covering my tracks because I knew that I was being watched. However, the throw-off methods learned as a street-smart youth proved to be valuable. For instance, I would do things like having my driver circle around the block twice before I got out anywhere.

Also, I would do things like, instead of me going inside an establishment immediately, I would send in Dante first. After he assured me, that the location was secure through a coded text message, I would then quickly enter the place in disguise. Sometimes I dressed up as an old man or sometimes I would look like a homeless person.

I am grateful to have someone like Dante as my right hand, he has continuously proven to be an asset in my operations. In addition, Dante was a former Special Forces Lieutenant, He is very equipped to manage tense situations with precision and accuracy should they arise. Thanks to current technology, I can run my companies remotely, therefore I do not have to be onsite every day to ensure things are running smoothly. Using the various modern technology devices allows me to stay on top of everything, every day.

Another key component of my team are my two impressive assistants. Twin sisters Tiara and Savannah are a dynamic duo! Both are recent honors graduates from the esteemed Prosser University. Both of them girls are exceptional in their own right and have a very bright future in front of them. Savannah has a degree in civil engineering like me, while Tiara holds a degree in cyber-security and data science.

They are both very sharp and efficient, and I am truly fortunate to have them on my team in addition to Dante. They assist me in ensuring that all my businesses are being run accordingly day-to-day.

Having such a dependable team allows me more time to do my research and follow up on any leads about the legend, while my businesses are still being managed. Taking Dante's advice, I hired a private former military security detail to monitor my parent's house as well as my grandparent's RV around the clock, just in case these strange people who were pursuing me got too desperate.

You always have to look out for your loved ones no matter what. I want my family to be protected while I am doing what I am doing. Although my father and my grandfather can definitely hold their own should someone ever try them, my thing is that they should not have to let someone who is a trained professional be the one to handle things if they should arise.

IX

COPPERVILLE REVELATIONS

Present Day Copperville, Ks

I continued my research. As time went on, I noticed that I started running into several brick walls gathering data surrounding the legend. Some of the local folks had either told me all that they knew, while others were not even aware of the story, so they had nothing to contribute. Despite this minor setback, I still was able to obtain a few more potential sources of information.

I traveled to a town north of Ewingston, situated on the banks of the Missouri River, called Copperville. This old, quaint town is said to be haunted. Growing up, I remember hearing a few eerie tales about this nearby town and some of the unexplained paranormal encounters and ghost stories rumored to have taken place there.

Once I arrived in Copperville, I drove around the town for a little while to get a feel for the place. I had not been up there in a while. Using a bogus identity, I checked into one of the local hotels for the night. The next day, after breakfast I headed over to the local jewelry store.

While there in Copperville, I came across something interesting that was directly related to those ten gold coins that I had found as a kid. Taking my parent's advice back then, I did manage to keep five of the gold coins from my find, while the rest were sold to a local jewel dealer there in Copperville.

To my astonishment, the same jeweler Mr. Tyler, still owned that jewelry store. He still had those two gold coins, after all these years! No doubt, these coins were indeed rare. There were these strange markings on the coins, I always wondered what these symbols actually meant. I never even thought to investigate what the unique symbols that were engraved on them meant. Honestly, at that age, I paid it no mind, I just wanted the fast cash at the time.

I found out through Mr. Tyler that those "unique" symbols were the monikers of the infamous Knights of the Golden Circle. Engraved on the coins were four pillars, with a 4-pointed star in the center.

Under a microscope, I noticed there were four words on each of the pillars (Union, Power, Legion, and AMR'N, which is an abbreviation of the word American) with 1859, the year of their inception was also engraved (Williams, Roush 2005). That was it! Mystery solved, at least that part of it was.

Using this newly found information I now knew why those strange people in them white vans were pursuing me. They turned out to be the descendants of a local faction of the KGC. They still wanted to find not only the remainder of their "lost" gold and also find the

Bomaki diamonds. Foolishly, they were thinking that I was going to be one to lead them to it, Nope, not a Chance bro! While I was in Copperville, I was able to find out some more historical information regarding my research through a few of its knowledgeable residents.

(Here goes an important history lesson. Take notes!)

Let's be completely honest here, the massive amounts of revenue that resulted from the enslavement of Foundational Black Americans created the wealth of the United States, Period! Some reports estimate the amount to be four billion dollars in today's currency, some would say it was more, and some say it was less.

Anyway, in the American South, slavery was the most prevalent, the entire economy was solely based on chattel slavery. Items such as tobacco, cotton, and indigo were three of the biggest moneymakers. The most common

forms of currency that were accumulated and hoarded,

were a combination of both US and Confederate money

and bonds, also including substantial amounts of solid gold

(Anderson, 1994).

Nine days after the end of the American Civil War,

on Good Friday, April 15, 1865, Confederate sympathizer,

and well-known stage actor John Wilkes Booth (Swanson,

2009) assassinated beloved President Abraham Lincoln at

Ford's Theater in Washington, D, C.

Booth's evil intention was to murder Lincoln's

entire presidential cabinet that night, which in his twisted

mind would be the catalyst to re-ignite the civil war and

therefore "avenge the South". Thankfully, however, his

dastardly plan failed miserably. This tragic event only

made Booth look like a traitor and a coward and he was a

wanted man.

After a long, twelve-day pursuit through Virginia

and Maryland, he, and another accomplice David Harold,

were eventually tracked down and killed by Union troops

at Garrett's Farm in Port Royal, Virginia (Swanson, 2009).

After this occurred, The KGC fell into disarray and

had to enact a new course of action. The KGC was forced

to restructure their organization and figure out where they

were going to hide all their ill-gotten treasures and money.

There were many places throughout America where

the KGC had allegedly hidden their loot, one of the many

rumored locations was Ewingston, Mo. There were even

rumors of KGC members staging fake funeral services with coffins filled with gold bars instead of deceased loved ones. This information proved to be a critical breakthrough in my research (Williams, Rousch, 2005).

(History lesson over, now Back to the story)

While I was there in Copperville, I knew I had to be cautious, because I knew the shady descendants of the KGC were still out there and were still heavy on my trail. One advantage that I had, was that no one knew that I was in Copperville. Dante was on his job, he had them thinking that I was still moving around First City performing my daily routines. That helped to buy me some time.

Acting on a tip from my Grandpa Julius, I went and visited a local elder by the name of Ole Bill Brown. He had to be every bit 80 years old or so, but despite his age, he was still sharp on all four corners! Ole Bill Brown was a dear old friend of my paternal grandfather, Julius. As we

sat on his porch, He began telling me stories about the

good ole days, back when he and my grandfather used to

run around Ewingston and Copperville together chasing

women and gambling all night in the local juke joints and

nightclubs.

Once I brought up the Legend of the Bomaki

diamonds, I noticed his energy instantly change. He

immediately got up from his chair and ushered me inside

his house. "Let's head inside," he said.

X

NO TURNING BACK

Present Day Copperville, KS, events took place July 1859

    Ole Bill Brown was a very insightful and humorous dude; I enjoyed conversing with him. I started to see why he and my granddad were old friends, they both shared the same old-school sense of humor while still commanding respect at the same time. They are two of a kind for sure!

    He said to me "Young brother, you need to be careful about who you speak to about that legend, especially around here," he said as he poured us two drinks of his exclusive Remy Martin Louis XIII cognac. He continued "You know they never did find those diamonds, and honestly, there are some people who would like to keep it that way because they think they are cursed". He was familiar with the KGC too and knew the things that they were capable of, especially if you got too close or

found out too much about them.

Not surprised, I replied, "Yes Sir, I'm aware of

them, I've heard that same thing a few times throughout

my research". "I am just trying to find out some more

info," I said to him, and he agreed with me, and we talked

some more.

After that brief conversation, Ole Bill Brown and I

began to compare notes of what I had discovered

throughout my research in addition to what he already

knew about the legend. I explained to him where my

research of the legend had hit a brick wall. He was able to

line me in on what he had heard took place regarding the

legend.

Passed down from three generations, his family's

account of the legend explained in detail how Maddie and

the others successfully escaped from the Stevenson plantation on the 4th of July of 1860. His family's account went a little something like this.

While the festivities were in full swing at the big house, under the cover of darkness, Maddie and the others quickly made their escape from the Stevenson plantation on their journey to be free.

They all took off and ran as fast as they could toward the timber, carrying the small number of belongings that they could carry along with them. Fortunately for them, their journey was not too far.

If they could find a safe passage across the river and they would be home free, literally. However, it was not going to be a cakewalk, there was a lot of ground for them to cover before daylight, so they had to run, run, and run as fast as they could with no interruptions.

Right before they took off on their journey toward freedom, the group made a stop near the Old Dominion cemetery to bid their deceased loved ones a final goodbye before they began their journey toward being finally free!

Meanwhile, back at the plantation, the party continued into the wee hours of the morning. During the drunken debauchery and all, nobody even noticed that three of the slaves had escaped.

Little did they know, there was one other person that also escaped, and that person was Hattie! Like Maddie, Hattie was also ready and willing to escape from the Stevenson plantation forever as well. She was fed up too and wanted to start a new life as a free woman.

Fortunately for Maddie and the others, during the early hours of the next morning, there was an unexpected severe thunderstorm with a devastating EF4 tornado wrapped inside of it. An EF4 tornado can have wind speeds between 116 and 200 miles per hour, very scary! very dangerously destructive!

Being that this is the Midwest, tornadoes are a common occurrence, especially during the Spring months. However, a tornado can also unexpectantly happen in the middle of summer, like in this case.

God was definitely on Maddie's side when this natural disaster occurred for sure! Fortunately, she and the others were able to take shelter inside a cave along the way. This cave was underneath a creek's waterfall in an area known as "The Groves" near the Old Dominion cemetery.

The storm was indeed severe! It was a deadly combination of a heavy downpour of rain, along with the 80 mph winds, constant lightning strikes, and thunder bursts that shook the ground. According to local historians, this was the worst tornado ever recorded in the area.

    While this massive tornado was happening, there was a lot of confusion and fear back at the Stevenson plantation. They were forced to end their party sooner than expected. Everyone there was scared, they thought they were all going to die at that moment. Whitney Stevenson nor his plantation overseers were able to take their daily head count of all the slaves to ensure that no one had escaped during the tornado. Everything was in disarray. People were panicking and praying to God that they would make it through.

After the tornado passed, the rain continued to fall

heavily, which began to flood the inside of the cave

where Maddie and the others were hiding. Because

of this, they were forced out of the cave and

continued running toward the river.

"Wow, this is very insightful, I can't believe

that I never heard this story before," I said to Ole

Bill Brown as he was telling me the story.

He shook his head and replied "Unfortunately, this

is where my family's recollection of the legend ends", he

told me. In closing, he did say that he heard, that Maddie,

Dwight, Ethel, Dovie Ann, and Hattie all were able to find

their way into Kansas with the help of the abolitionists

working near the river.

"Sorry young brother, that's all I know, hope this

helps you with your research," he said to me as I was

leaving his house. I thanked him and headed back home. Yes, the information he provided had indeed helped but I still was not satisfied, I knew there had to be more to the story. When I returned to Free City from my trip up to Copperville, I scheduled an emergency meeting with my team.

This meeting took place at an undisclosed location outside of Ewingston. I wanted us all to compare notes and discuss strategies moving forward. It was late at night when we arrived at our location, so we called it night and planned on meeting early the next morning.

Along with Dante, my two trusty assistants Tiara and Savannah were immensely helpful in providing me with some vital unknown details about the legend of the Bomaki diamonds and what became of Maddie and the others.

Present Day Free City, Ks, events took place July 1859

According to their research, Maddie and her group of escaped slaves had to split up once they reached the river. The word had gotten out that five slaves from the Stevenson Plantation and one from the Bruner plantation had recently escaped and were now on the loose. Wanted posters with a five-hundred-dollar reward along with descriptions of each of the escapees were posted everywhere throughout St. Georges County. False rumors spread quickly among the locals that Maddie and her group were armed and dangerous, which they were not, I mean how could they be? They were slaves, and slaves could not carry any type of weapons.

Once they reached the river, everyone hugged and said their goodbyes to each other and wished each other well in their travels. After this, they all split up and headed

in different directions. Luckily, Maddie was able to find

some of those Black Freedmen that I mentioned earlier

working on the docks near the river.

Remembering what young Dovie Ann had told her

earlier, she cautiously replied using the code word "blazing

out", responding to one of the Freedmen that had spoken to

her first. This Freedman was a brave young man by the

name of Cassius. He instantly recognized Maddie's intent

and gave the signal to the others nearby. After this, Maddie

was in the process of being concealed inside the bottom of

a river steamboat.

Then all of the sudden, the ruthless Kilgore along

with two of his cronies appeared, out of nowhere! "Get

that black bitch! Do not let her get away!" shouted

Kilgore, as he and two of his men sprinted across the river

dock toward the steamer as it was leaving the river dock.

Just then, Maddie's adrenaline kicked in at that very

moment. It was Fight or Flight! Having to make a split-

second decision while being chased and shot at, she

instantly dove into the rushing rapids of the Big Muddy.

Keep in mind, that there had just been a massive

tornado and thunderstorm, so the river was very

overflooded. There was a lot of debris such as large trees

and logs floating down the river, making it extremely

dangerous.

Luckily for the intrepid Maddie, the survival

lessons, and instincts, she had learned as a child had now

come in handy. She was able to avoid her captors, as well

as drowning, and she successfully escaped. Kilgore and his cohorts were enraged! "Kill that nigger bitch" he yelled at his men.

He started cussing and stomping his feet on the dock. His men then started shooting aimlessly into the river, hoping to hit her. Because the debris floating in the river made it nearly impossible for them to see if they had indeed shot her as they were intending to do. "Damnit, I think she got away!" Shouted an angry Kilgore as he angrily stomped across the large river dock.

Kilgore knew that most slaves were insured so killing one of them would cost him money, but he did not care, as far as he was concerned "a good black is a dead black", especially the ones seeking freedom, no way! Not on his watch.

After the news broke that Maddie and the others escaped from the Stevenson plantation, Whitney Stevenson was furious. He and a few of his men went to the river docks and confronted Kilgore. Tempers flared and after a heated exchange of cuss words and blame, a gunfight broke out between the two entourages. When it was over Kilgore and three of his men lay dead on the dock after being shot to death by Whitney Stevenson and his men.

XI

WHEN THE DUST SETTLED

Present Day Free City, Ks, events took place July 1859

My team and I were able to piece together the story of what happened to everyone after their escape. Maddie hid out in and around Kansas for about a year or so after her escape. She became like a Midwestern version of Harriet Tubman. She helped the Freedman on the docks free a lot of fugitive slaves.

Eventually, Maddie made her way back north to present-day Carson, Nebraska, and found what was left of her village. She was never seen or heard from again. Some believe that she continued into the West and disappeared into the mountains of Colorado.

Dwight and Ethel were also able to avoid capture after their escape. With the assistance of some abolitionists, they were both able to obtain some makeshift freedom papers, should anyone question them. They eventually made their way up north into Canada, where they built a beautiful home and raised a large family.

Young Dovie Ann was also able to make her way into freedom. She became a conductor on the Underground Railroad and worked as a Union spy during the Civil War.

She later relocated to California, where she and her husband Thomas, started a remarkably successful avocado farm in the Central Valley. There they raised thirteen children, seven girls, and six boys. They had more than enough help maintaining their farm! Rumor has it their descendants still operate or have a piece of the ownership in many of the modern avocado farms in that area to this day!

And finally, we cannot forget about the brave Hattie. She proved to be a real-life local hero and anti-slavery champion until her untimely murder a few months after her escape. "The details surrounding her death are sketchy,"

Tiara said to me as I gazed out the window into the morning light, sipping my coffee.

"Yeah, I can't believe that she had gone through all of those things, risking her life on all those occasions, just for her to be killed so easily, it doesn't make no sense," I said. She then continued with the information from her sources. Hattie was found dead from an alleged poisoning in an abandoned house in a small town out in western Kansas. That got me thinking, I was willing to bet that the KGC folks probably played a role in her demise, and the legend of the Bomaki diamonds could possibly be solved if we continued in our quest to find the truth!

After our team meeting, I headed back to where it all started, Ewingston. I had some more searching to do. Once I returned to Ewingston, I began looking in and around the Old Dominion cemetery looking for more clues.

At first, we tried to be cautious and move discreetly as I am sure we were being watched, not only by the descendants of the KGC but also by the townspeople as well. After a few days had passed by, word spread around town that we were there searching for the diamonds.

I did not mind though because I figured that we could be onto something big! I even called the local news channel, not only for the exposure but also for visibility just in case anyone wanted to harm any of us during our search efforts.

With special permission from the County Commissioner Mr. Anthonni Wayman, who owed me a favor, my team and I began the excavation. Of course, we were not allowed to dig up any of the coffins, as that would be illegal unless authorized by him or another ranked official.

After about a week or so of searching the grounds and digging around the Old Dominion Cemetery in Ewingston, unfortunately, we came up empty-handed. The only things we found were some old scrap items and junk, basically garbage.

Since our search had become more or less a lost cause, I went ahead and called it off with my team. I also sent out a press release to the local media that we were inconclusive despite our best search efforts.

I then packed my bags and returned back home to Free City and got on with my life. It felt good to be back home and back to business. After a few months, all the fanfare about the search for the legend of the Bomaki diamonds had ceased.

One night as I was finishing dinner, I received an urgent text message on my cellphone. The message came from an Ewingston area code, so I figured it must be someone I knew. Who is this from? I wondered. The message read in all caps "MEET ME NEAR THE GROVE AT DUSK, DO NOT BE LATE". I was on it! I knew exactly where that was. This could be the breakthrough that I was looking for!

According to my research, I found that after the civil war ended in 1865, the Stevenson plantation fell on tough times. With no free labor source to generate the revolving profit and wealth, they had grown accustomed to; the plantation went under. Whitney Stevenson decided to relocate his family back to Louisiana.

After this, the property sat vacant for many years, until a local doctor who was a relative of the Stevenson family purchased the property and turned it into a bed and breakfast. Nowadays it operates as a historical museum, in which, ironically, I have a piece of the ownership.

Separating the grounds of the Stevenson plantation and the Old Dominion Cemetery is a densely populated wooded area of Sycamore trees known to the locals as the "The Grove".

The folks that had been spying on me were still out there, I was sure of it, so I was still being cautious of where I went and to whom I talked. During this time, I relied more on Dante, Tiara, and Savannah to make sure my daily business rounds were being taken care of. I covertly slipped away and went to meet this mysterious person who had contacted me.

In light of recent events, I was in a high state of paranoia, so I was heavily armed, just in case things went awry. I did not want to get caught slipping. I reached the grove just before dusk, as instructed by the stranger that texted me.

XII

HIDDEN SECRETS

Present Day Ewingston, Mo

After about ten minutes or so of waiting around, I noticed a dark figure appear out of nowhere. It was an old woman. She was wearing all black and had a large hood and veil covering her face. I approached her slowly and tried to get a better look at her face. "Don't look at me" she said in a raspy voice as I approached her. "All right" I replied as I looked away. She then said, "Take This" and handed me a folded-up piece of paper. She then quickly disappeared back into the trees.

I left the grove immediately, got with my team, and went up to Copperville to reveal what that mysterious woman I met in the Groves had given to me. With the help of my team and Ole Bill Brown, I was able to decipher the symbols and characters on the document, which turned out to be a map.

The language in which the text was written on the map is referred to as Tutnese, or TUT, which was a secret language created by Foundational Black American slaves.

This was done at a time when it was against the law for any slave to learn and read and write (McIIwain, 1995).

For example, A, B, and C would be pronounced as "ay-bub-cuc". I cannot lie it was a little difficult to understand it at first, but eventually, we were able to figure out what the map was trying to say to us. The map had many symbols and characters, including a large house with a cemetery next to it. Next to this, there was something that resembled some sort of tunnel on the map. This was the area between the Stevenson Plantation and the Old Dominion Cemetery. I was so excited! Could I finally be close to finally solving the mystery of the Legend of the Bomaki diamonds? Maybe? Hopefully!

Then all the sudden, out of nowhere, a series of gunshots broke out, "BLAP, BLAP, BLAP, BLAP, BLAP" "Get down!" I yelled as bullets whizzed through the windows and walls like a sharp knife cutting through

butter!

They must have let off about twenty rounds at us.

Amid all the bullets flying and glass shattering, it almost

seemed like everything was moving in slow motion. It was

a beautiful nightmare in real life!

After all the shots ended, I went and checked on

everybody to make sure no one had been hit by any of the

many bullets fired at us, fortunately for us, no one got shot.

Once I knew that the team was all safe, Dante and I

instantly grabbed a few fully automatic weapons, jumped

in his truck, and took off.

Luckily for us, Dante noticed a strange white van

with tinted windows had been circling the block several

times before the shots rang out. We left in the same

direction that the van was heading in which was south.

With Dante's expert driving skills, we were able to catch up with the white van.

After a suspenseful car chase on the highway, involving us trading gunshots back and forth at high speeds had ensued, Dante quickly swerved over and ran their vehicle off a steep embankment. As we were driving away, we heard a loud crash sound followed by a very loud BOOM sound! Not sure if they died or not, but honestly, we did not care, we got ourselves out of there as fast as possible, and thankfully for us, there were no witnesses around.

The next morning, as I was watching the local First City news, I expected to see a story about the car chase and crash that had happened the night before on the highway south of Copperville. But there was no mention of it whatsoever, it was like it never even happened.

Hmm? I figured that whoever it was that was shooting at us was more than likely part of a larger scheme that did not want to be exposed, and the people that were sent to kill us were some of their expendables. Regardless, I knew now more than ever that we had to be more careful, incredibly careful! I then instructed my team to move with caution and to lay low until I gave them a signal.

After a week or so, I reached out to my team and let them know that I would be needing their assistance real soon. I did not indicate when that would be, "Just be ready", is all I told them. I let a few weeks pass by and started to notice things had pretty much gone back to normal, and there did not appear that anyone was trying to follow us anymore.

I continued with my daily routines, and we did not speak about the legend whatsoever around the office. After

I felt that things had cooled down, I sent out a text to my team in the Tutnese language that I recently had learned.

The message read "Gug-Rug-Oh-Vuv-E" which translates to GROVE with specific instructions to meet me at a specific section of the groves before dawn in two days. I told them to move very discreetly and to tell no one about it.

Two days later, just like clockwork, my team and I arrived at the requested location, ready for action. Over the time that we were inactive, I thoroughly studied the map that was given to me by the mysterious lady I had met up with at the Grove and tried my best to understand what it meant. Come to find out, this map was an actual interpretation of the grounds of the Stevenson Plantation. I found out that there were some local notable nearby spots on it, including a previously unknown place called "The Underpass". What was that? I wondered.

XIII

NOT ALWAYS OBVIOUS

Present Day Ewingston, Mo

This "UnderPass" that I am referring to, was the place in which, Maddie, Dwight, Ethel, Dovie Ann, and Hattie all took cover during that disastrous tornado that occurred on July 5, 1859. Over the years, this place had been completely hidden due to the growing vegetation and was all but forgotten about by the locals.

The map led us to the right to where the underpass was! Not wanting to bring any attention to what we were doing, we began digging with

shovels. Yes, it was a chore, but it was a lot quieter

than us using some loud machinery and drawing

some unwanted attention from the locals.

After about an hour or so of digging in the

dark, we discovered within the waterfall, that there

was indeed an underpass that led on for several

miles. Using LED lanterns and flashlights, we

ducked down and slowly made our way into this

tunnel. It was creepy, cold, and dark. It also had that

old mildewy smell like an old basement or

crawlspace.

After a while, we finally reached the end of

it." Damnit, That's it? "Dante said as the path ended

at a dirt wall. Since we did not find anything

throughout the entire passageway, we decided to head back to the entrance and call it quits.

Just then, my intuition kicked in, something told me that I needed to check out the map one more time. "Hold Up a second," I said, holding my index finger up. While observing the map, I noticed there was a symbol inside of what resembled some sort of tunnel. The symbol was a tiny red triangle located in the center of the tunnel. I then took out one of my smaller shovels and started digging into the sidewall of the underpass in the area that resembled the location on the map. At first, I did not feel or see anything, then all of the sudden I felt the small shovel hit something solid. It felt like a box.

"I think I found something," I said. I continued digging away and eventually was able to free the box from its earthen hiding place. I could instantly tell the box was old, but it was still in decent shape though, I immediately

placed the old box inside my bag. Also, behind the old

wooden box was a gunny sack, it was very heavy, and I

wondered what was in it.

After this, we all high-tailed it out of there as fast as

we could! When I got back home, I opened the old box, it

was indeed old, it had a very mildewy smell like an old

basement or crawl space. After carefully removing the

outer edges, I was able to get finally get to what was inside

the box, which contained a small brown burlap bag. Inside

the bag were, you guessed it, there were approximately one

thousand shiny green diamonds! I was astonished, I could

not believe my eyes. The legend was true! My grandfather

Julius was right! The mystery of whether the Bomaki

diamonds were real or not had finally been solved, they did exist!

There I was holding onto a piece of history. People had died over these diamonds; people had even attempted to kill us over them. It was a crazy and exciting feeling all at once! I knew I still had to be careful because the descendants of the KGC were still out there on the prowl.

In addition to finding the diamonds, in the gunny sack were twenty-two bars of Confederate solid gold with the letters "CSA" stamped on them! What the KGC nor the press knew, is that we now actually found the diamonds and some of the supposedly "lost" rebel gold! I kept everything we discovered between myself and my team and told them not to tell anyone, not even their close friends or family.

I also was able to find out some information about something I mentioned earlier. Remember Smoky and Reno, those two terrifying Dobermans that roamed the Old Dominion cemetery at night? Well, come to find out their owners happened to be some of the descendants of the KGC, you know, those idiots that have been trailing me.

They knew there was buried treasure nearby the cemetery. They had been secretly searching for it. Their sick, twisted reasoning for letting those vicious attack dogs roam around the cemetery at night was to deter anyone from searching for it too, while they were searching for it, which happened to be at night!

I can remember one night in particular in which, one of my friends and I had a close encounter with those two demon dogs. We were riding our bikes to his house for a sleepover. I remember being so excited because my parents had just bought me a new bike, it was a white Schwinn Predator BMX. Anyway, it was right at sunset so we were pedaling as fast as we could to get to his house and beat the streetlights coming on.

We both knew that if the streetlights came on before we got there, we would have some explaining to do, and depending on how that went, it could mean no sleepover for us.

As we were passing by this big old white and green house on a corner, the next thing we knew, we heard the sound of a chain-breaking "Bink!" followed by the terrorizing sound of paws on the pavement coming toward us. "Oh, Shit! Here they Come," I said to my friend in a fearful tone. And sure enough, those two evil muts appeared out of the darkness. All we could see was their eyes glowing in the moonlight. They were barking, growling, and coming at us at full speed! "You betta pedal boy," I said as we took off on our bikes to try and outrun them.

Fortunately for us, this house had a large yard, so the street was quite a distance from behind the house where they were coming from. We took off, at break-neck speed, pedaling, steering, hearts racing, giving it all we had trying to get away from those two.

Once they were on us, they were on us, in hot pursuit! It was like I could feel them breathing down my back, just waiting for one of us to make a mistake and we were going to be their doggy dinner that night!

Luckily for us, we rode our bikes all over Ewingston since we were kids, so we knew all of the shortcuts, paths, and other different routes to lose anything or anyone that was chasing us.

Using those evasive skills combined with our quick instincts, we both were able to shake those two. We quickly made it to my homie's house, safe, out of breath, sweating, hearts beating a hundred miles an hour, but safe though. "Whew! That was close I said." "Hell, yeah it was Juke" my homie replied.

Unfortunately for Smoky and Reno, their cruel master's bad karma of teaching them to be mean caught up with them. The two dogs attacked a little girl one night and were immediately put down (shot) by the little girl's father.

Eventually, that led to a lawsuit in which the owners of Smoky and Reno were sued by that little girl's parents. The parents of the little girl won, and they were awarded a considerable sum of money from the dog's owners.

Honestly, I am no fan of harming animals, but I wish someone had put them down years ago. As a kid, I remember my parents and my friend's parents telling us that we had to be in the house before the streetlights came on, with no exceptions. And that night we really found out why.

XIV

PAST, PRESENT, AND FUTURE

Zurich, Switzerland & Bo, Sierra Leone Present Day

Later on, that same night after we found the diamonds and gold, Tiara, Savannah, Dante, and I chartered a private jet and flew over to Zurich, Switzerland. Our mission was to meet up with a world-renowned diamond appraiser named Yuri. After a long 12-hour flight plus a layover in London, we finally reached Zurich.

After a few days of being there and some negotiations with Yuri, the diamond appraiser, history was finally made! Let us just say no one from my team or their families will ever have to work again! As far as the gold is concerned, it also ended up in its rightful place!

Considering our recently found fortune, I knew in my heart that I had to do what was right. We left

Switzerland and made our way down to Sierra Leone.

With the assistance of some of the locals, we were able to

find the village of Bo, near the Sewa River.

Once there, we met with the elders of the village and

respectfully returned some of the Bomaki diamonds to

their rightful owners, the descendants of Prince Bomaki.

We were all fascinated and consumed with the West

African culture during our stay in Sierra Leone. The

people there are so beautiful, and they welcomed us with

open arms. We enjoyed the food, customs, and vibrant

traditional clothing. I enjoyed speaking with many of the

elders as well as the young people of that great nation!

They were able to give us some valuable insight and

history into who we are as a people before we were

captured and sold into slavery in America. Acting on a tip

from an associate, I went and visited the Door of No

Return Museum in Dakar, Senegal. Also known as the

"House of Slaves," the museum is a memorial to the

horrors of the Trans-Atlantic Slave trade. I wondered how

many people had come through that door, never to return.

Eventually, I made my way over to the west coast of

Sierra Leone. Once I made it there, I took a long walk on

the beach. During my walk, I was profoundly overcome

with a sense of relief as well as fulfillment.

Being in the birthplace of civilization was surreal, it

gave me a real sense of pride! I was spellbound knowing

all the things that my people had endured and despite this,

were still able to thrive. At the same time, I also felt a deep sadness mixed with compassion inside my soul. What a terrible tragedy!

It was so hard to imagine what took place there, once upon a time. I wonder what was on the minds of the African captives, as they were bound in chains and forcibly marched to the coast, to be loaded onto the awaiting European slave ships.

These brave souls had no idea what was in store for them. They had no idea where they were going, what was going to happen to them, or if they would ever see their families and villages again.

Some of the captives were fortunate to survive the perilous Middle Passage, however many perished along the way. Their bodies were thrown overboard to become feed for the sharks. Rumor has it that the great white sharks in the Atlantic Ocean began to follow the slave ships in order to get food, and that food was human flesh.

All those thoughts began to weigh heavily on my conscious. I was profoundly grateful that my team and I had finally solved this long-unsolved mystery. It felt amazing for us to be returning the Bomaki diamonds to their rightful owners in their rightful place!

Humbled by the many awakening experiences in our culture that we all shared while in the Motherland, we decided to set up shop there and make it one of our satellite sites. It was a new beginning for us, and we embraced it wholeheartedly!

REFERENCE LIST

1.) Kerrihard, Bowen, <u>America's Civil War</u>, March 1999

2.)Britannica, The Editors of Encyclopedia.
"Fugitive Slave Acts". Encyclopedia

*Britannica, 23 Jul. 2020,
https://www.britannica.com/event/Fugitive-
Slave-Acts. Accessed 7 June 2022.*

3.) https://www.blackpast.org/african-american-
history/concepts-african-american-history/the-
black-maroons-of-florida-1693-1850/, Otis
Alexander, Blackpast.org, April 06, 2022

4.) William, Roy Dr., Roush, D. PhD., _The Mysterious
and Secret Order of the Knights of the Golden Circle_,
Front Line Press, 2005

5.) Anderson, Dr. Claude, _Black Labor, White Wealth:
The Search for Power and Economic Justice_,
Powernomics Corp of America, Duncan & Duncan,
August 1, 1994, 250 pgs.

6.) Bowen, Morgan, _How Gabriel Prosser Planned What
Would Have Been The Largest Slave Rebellion In
American History_,
www.allthatsinsteresting.com/gabriel-Prosser,
December 09, 2021.

7.) Horwitz, Tony, Oreskes, Dan _Midnight Rising: John
Brown and the Raid that Sparked the Civil War_,
Macmillan Audio, October 25, 2011, 11 hours, and 5
minutes.

8.) Diouf, Sylviane, McCormick, Chante,' _Slavery's Exiles: The Story of the American Maroons_, Tantor Audio, May 31, 2022.

9.) Swanson, James L., _Chasing Lincoln's Killer_, Scholastic Press, Illustrated edition (February 1, 2009).

10.)   McIlwain, Gloria, _TUT Language_, Tut Language Company, January 1, 1995.

11.)   Nasheed, Tariq, _Foundational Black American Race Baiter_, King Flex Entertainment, December 1, 2021.

FEWELL MEDIA

PRINTED IN THE UNITED STATES OF AMERICA